This Wonderful Coloring Book Belongs To:

ISBN: 9788195484737

Horse

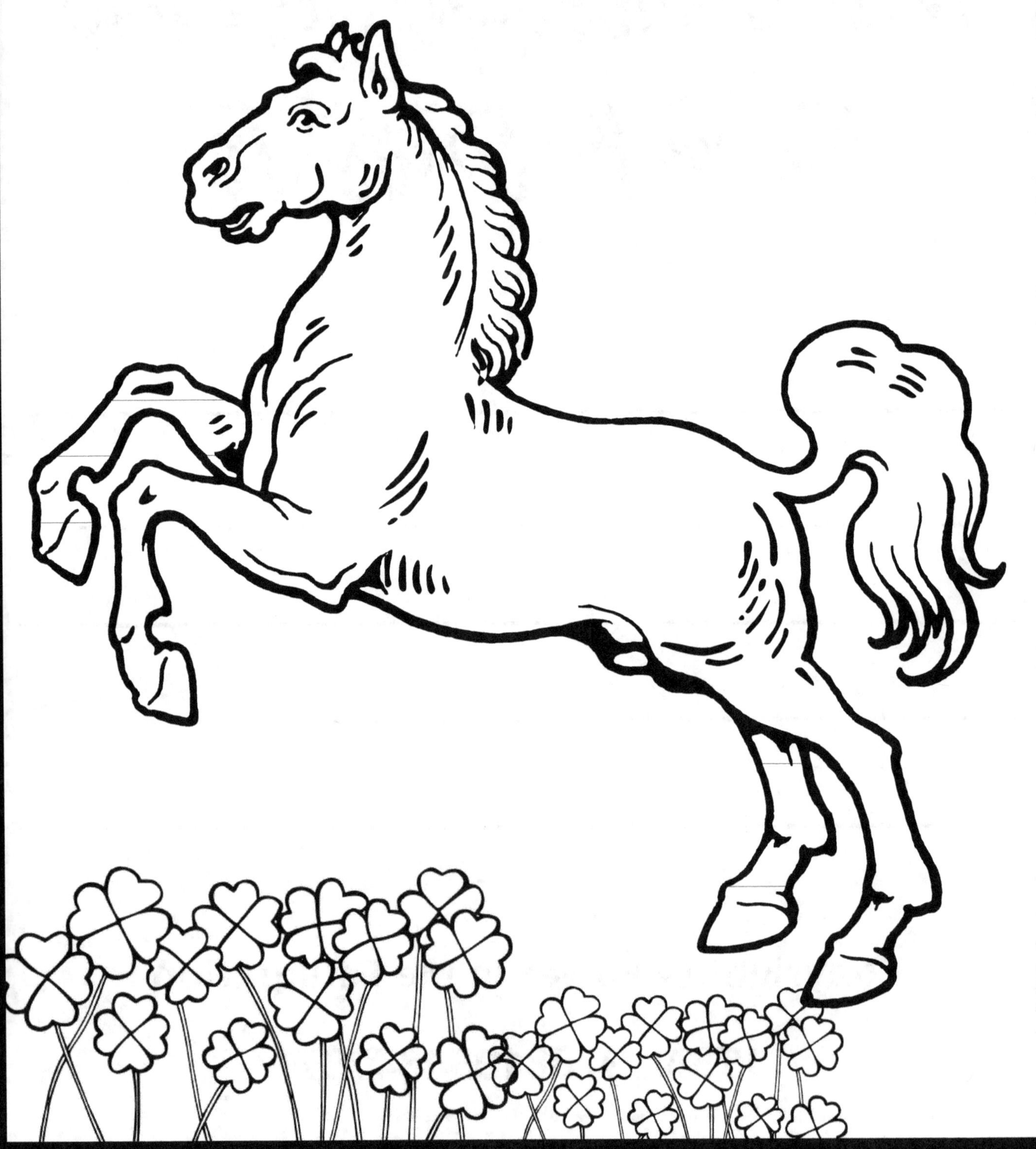

Rabbit

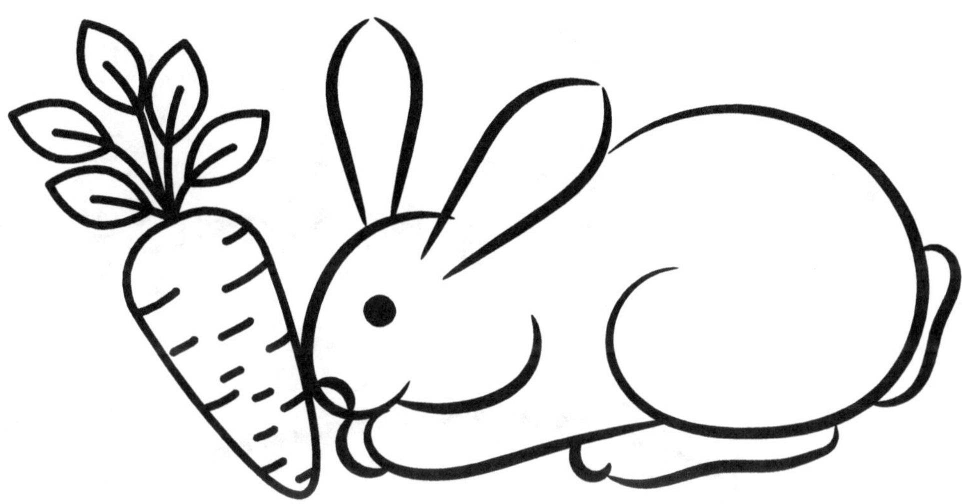

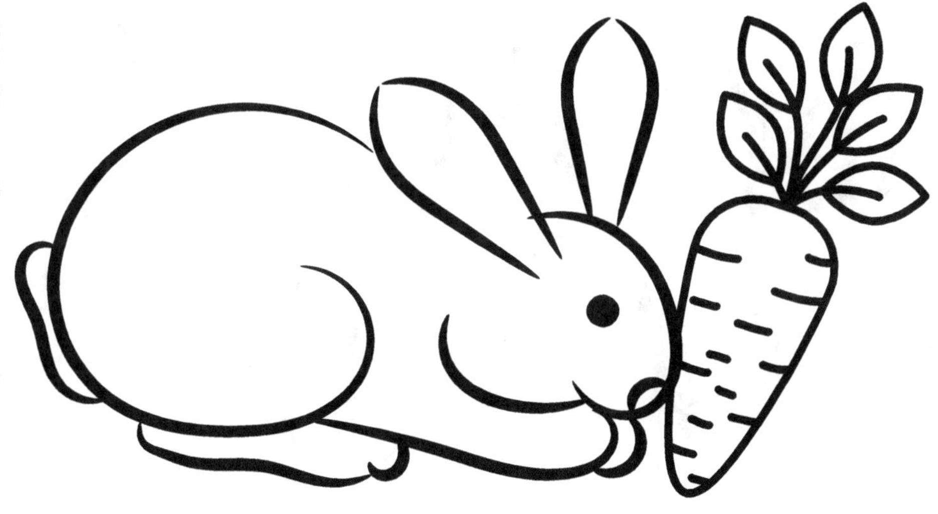

Elephant

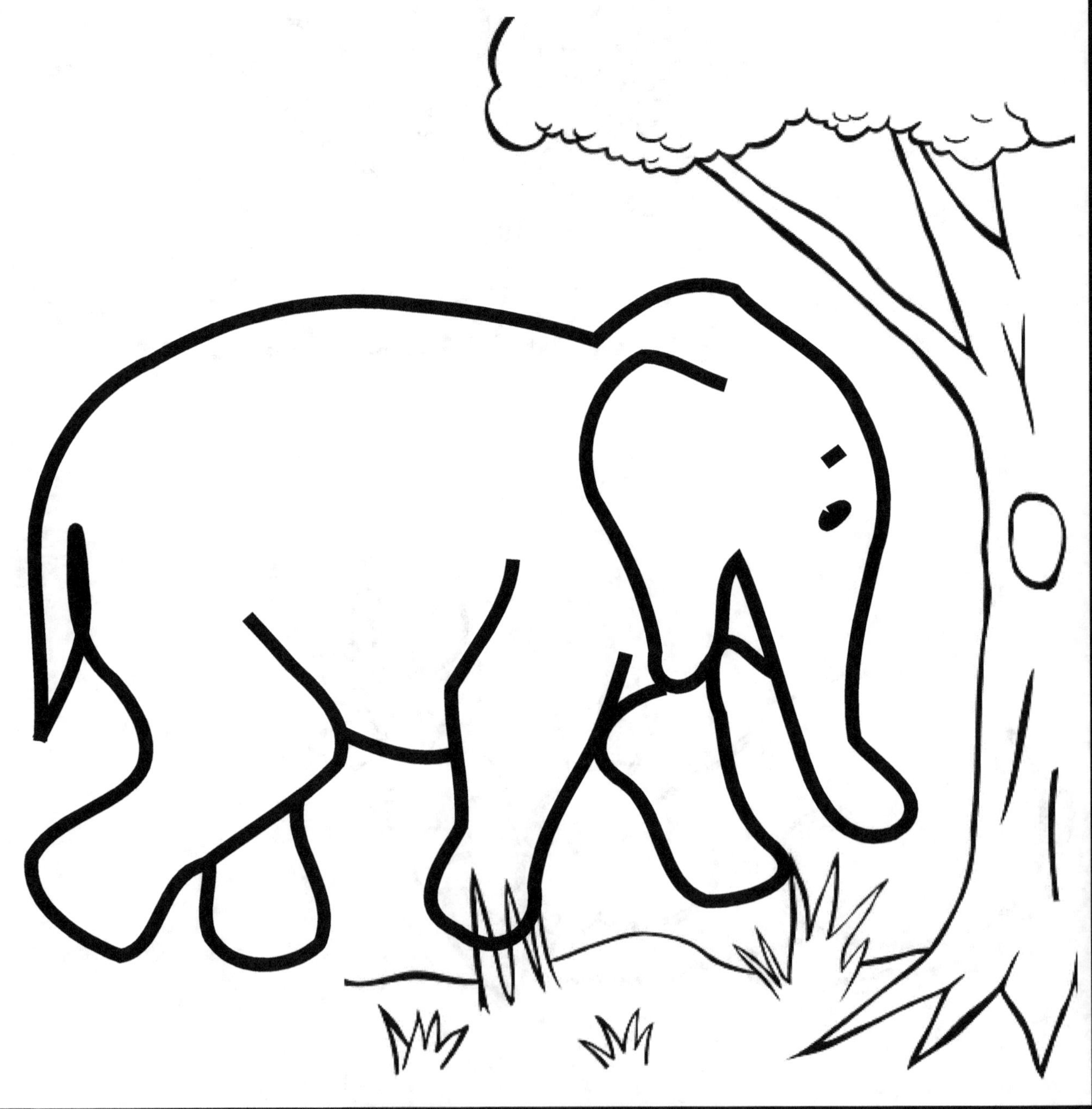

Giraffe

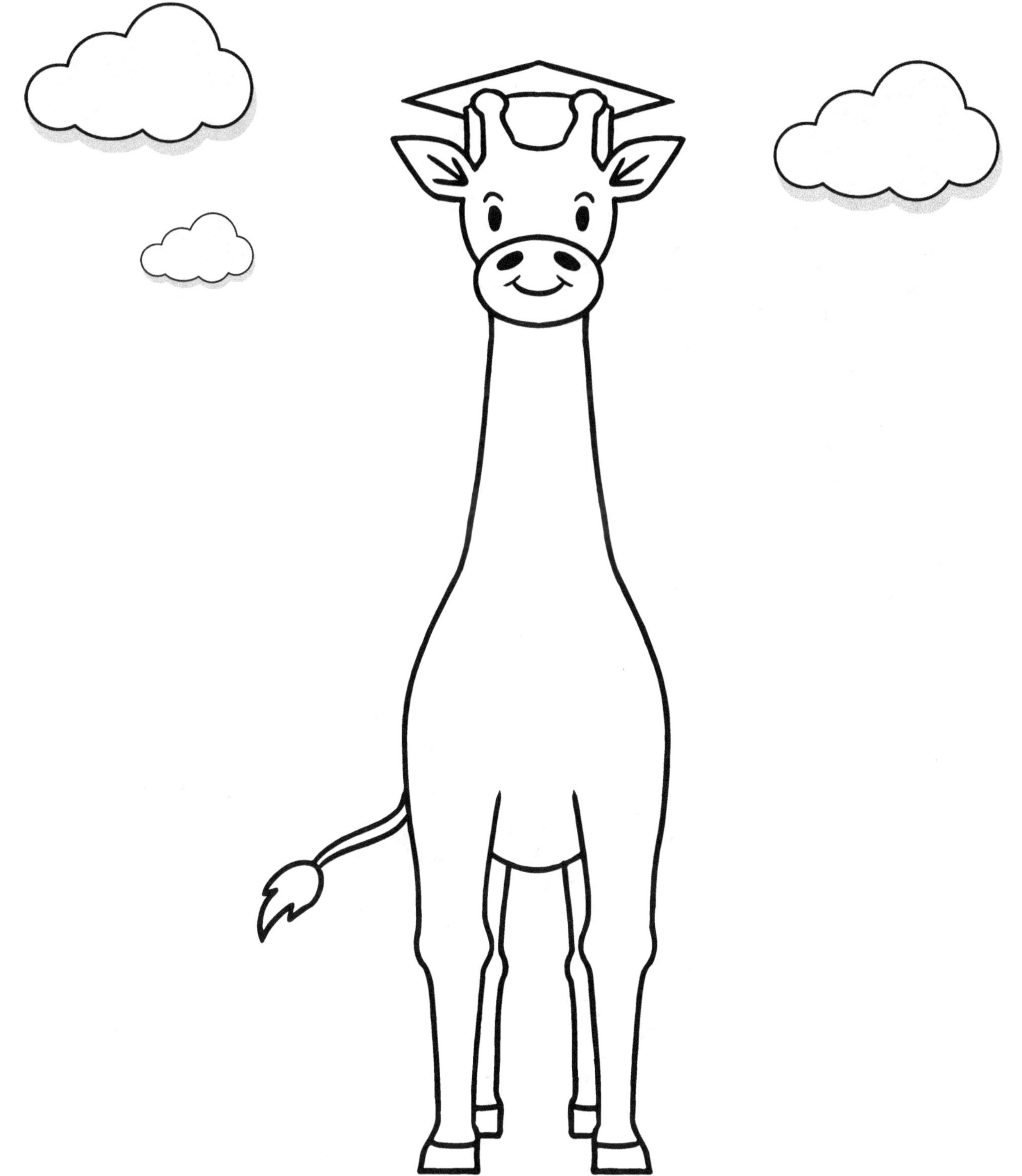

Cat

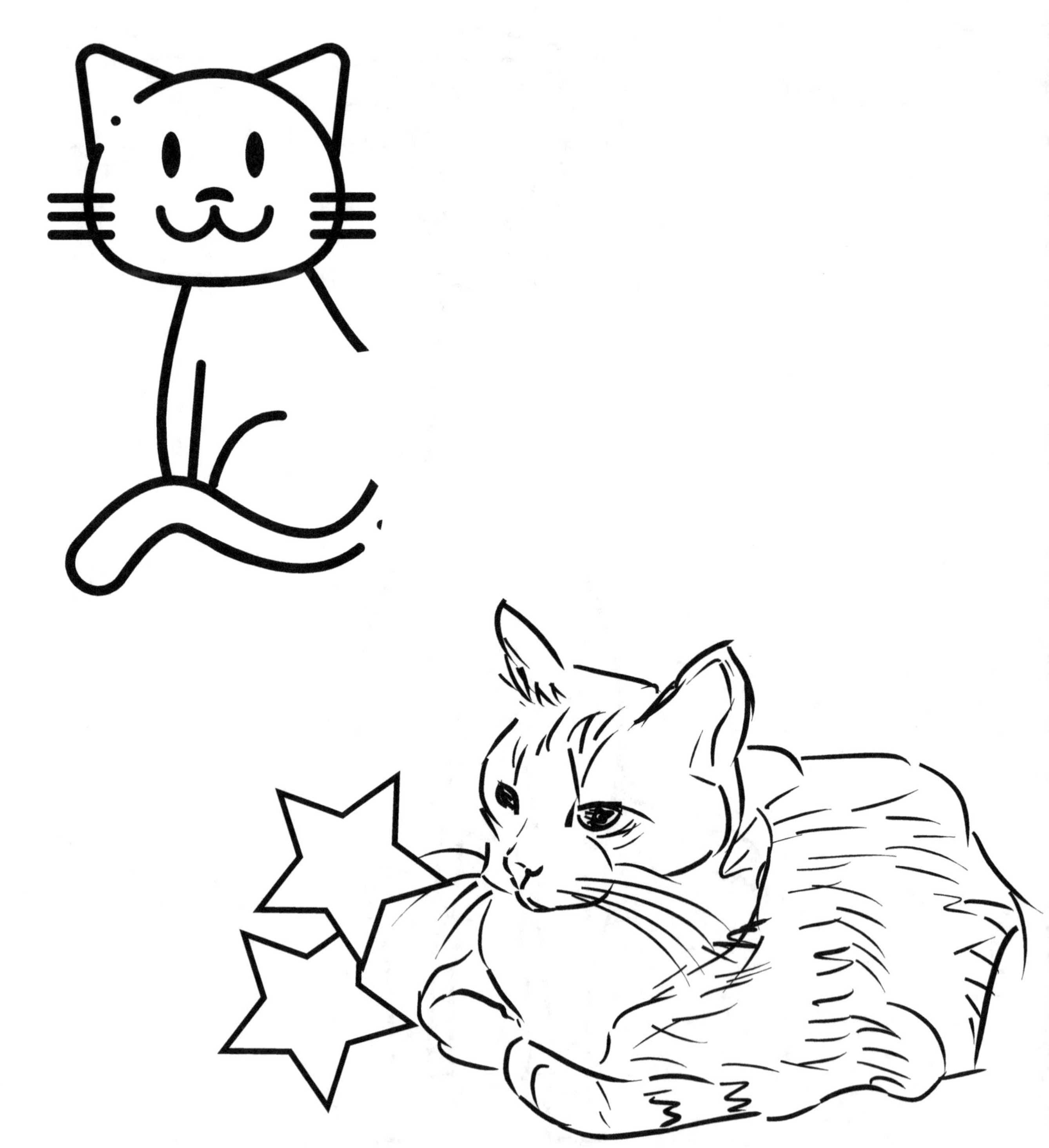

Puppy

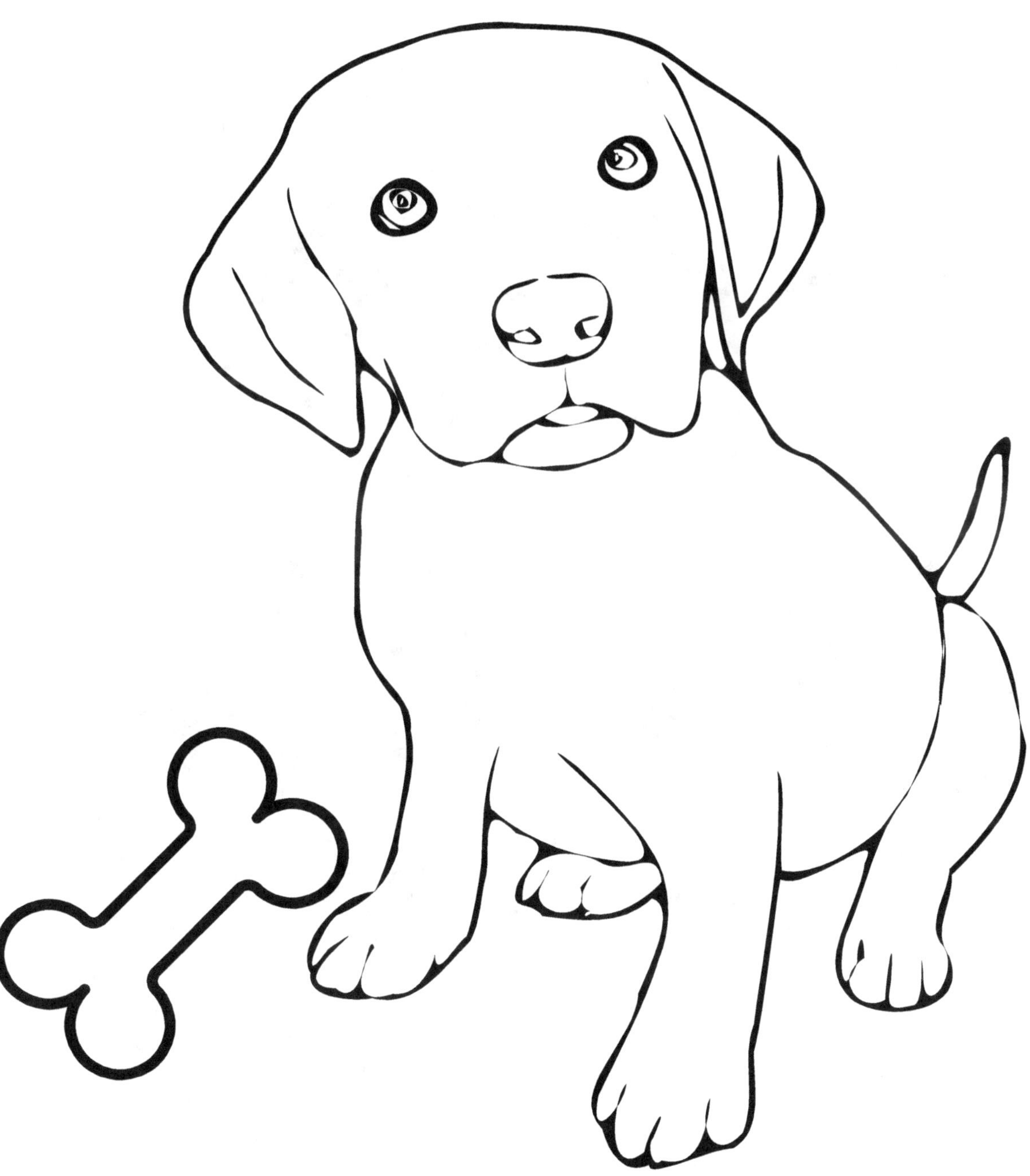

Monkey

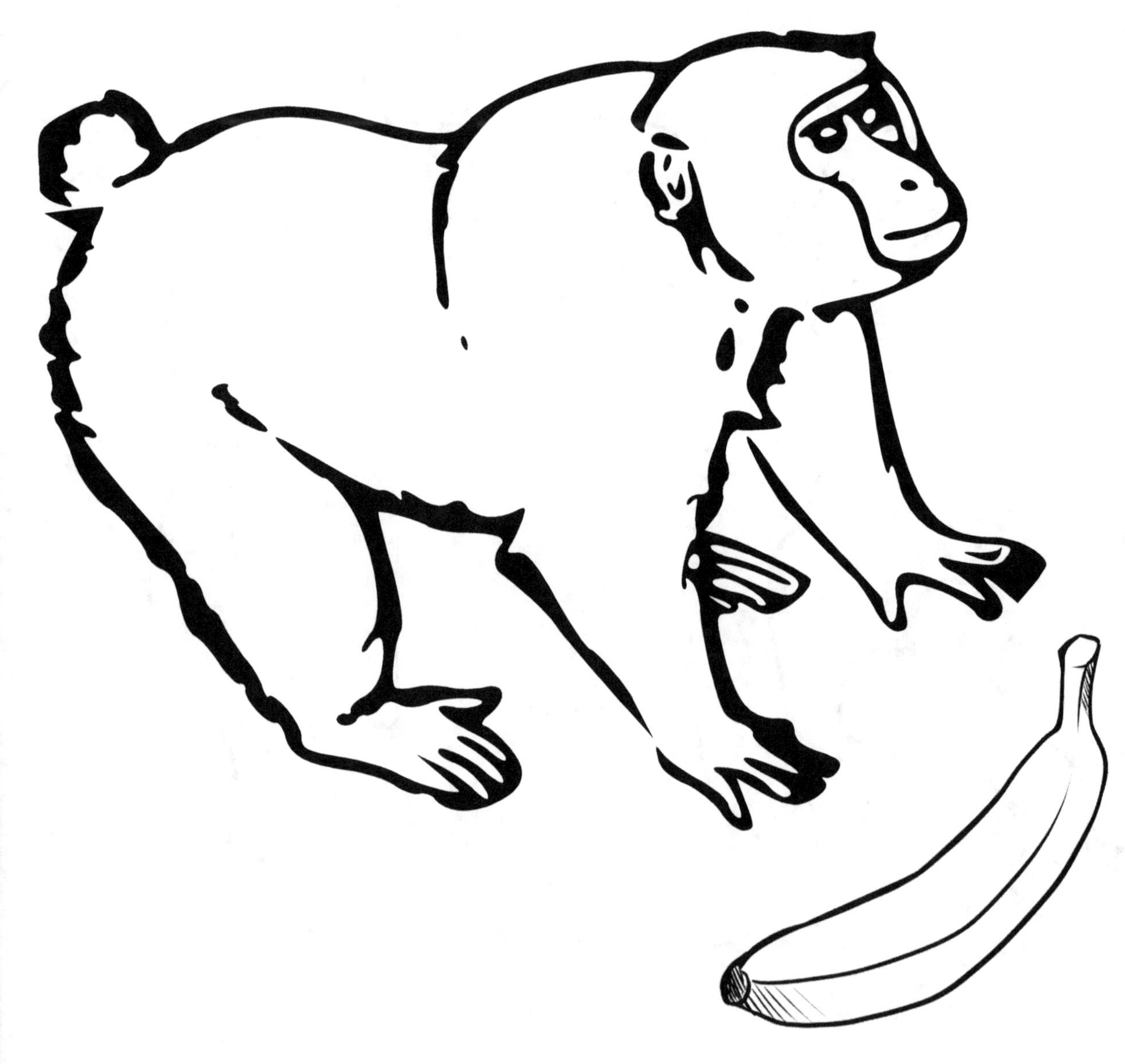

Donkey

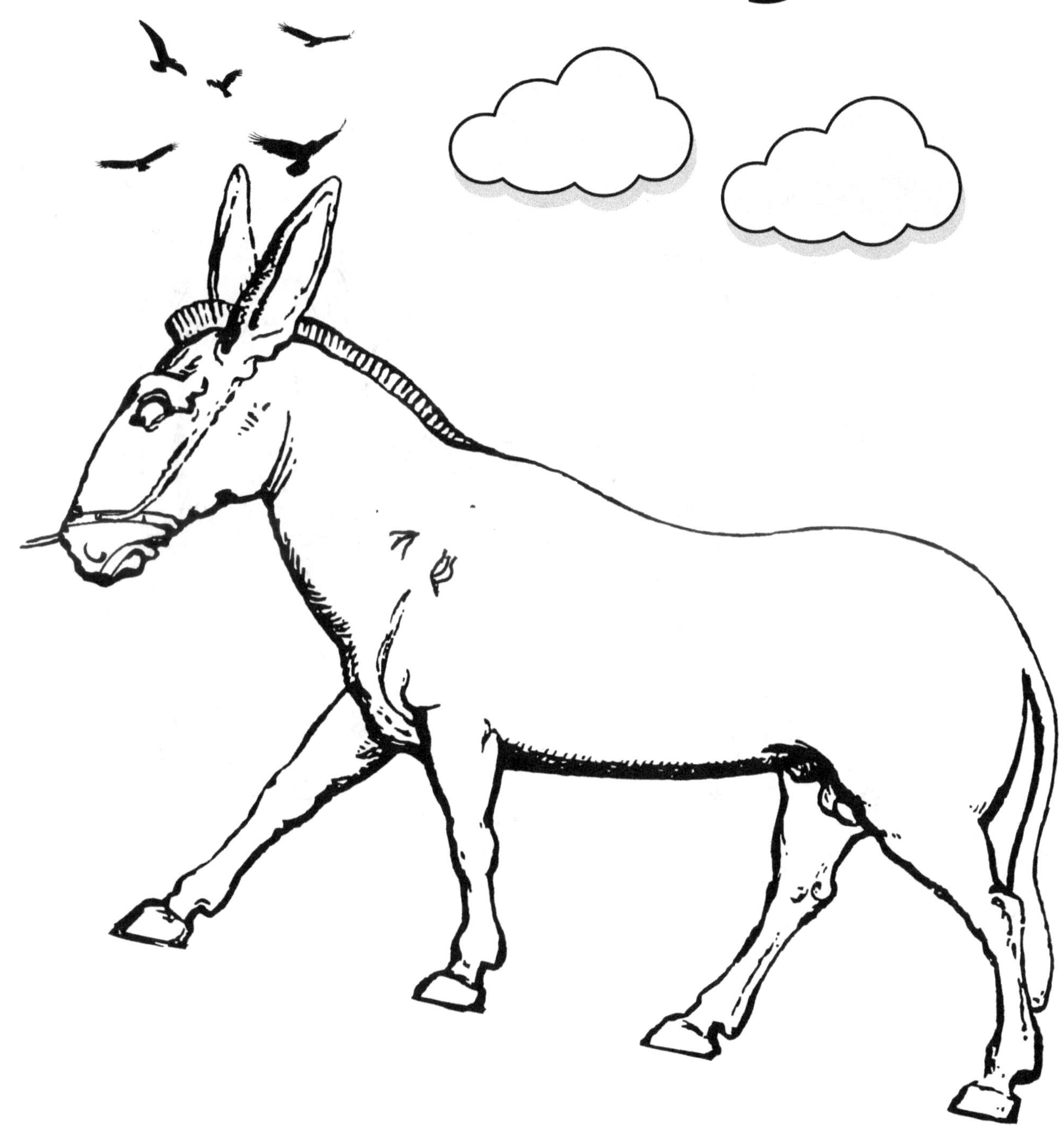

Buffalo

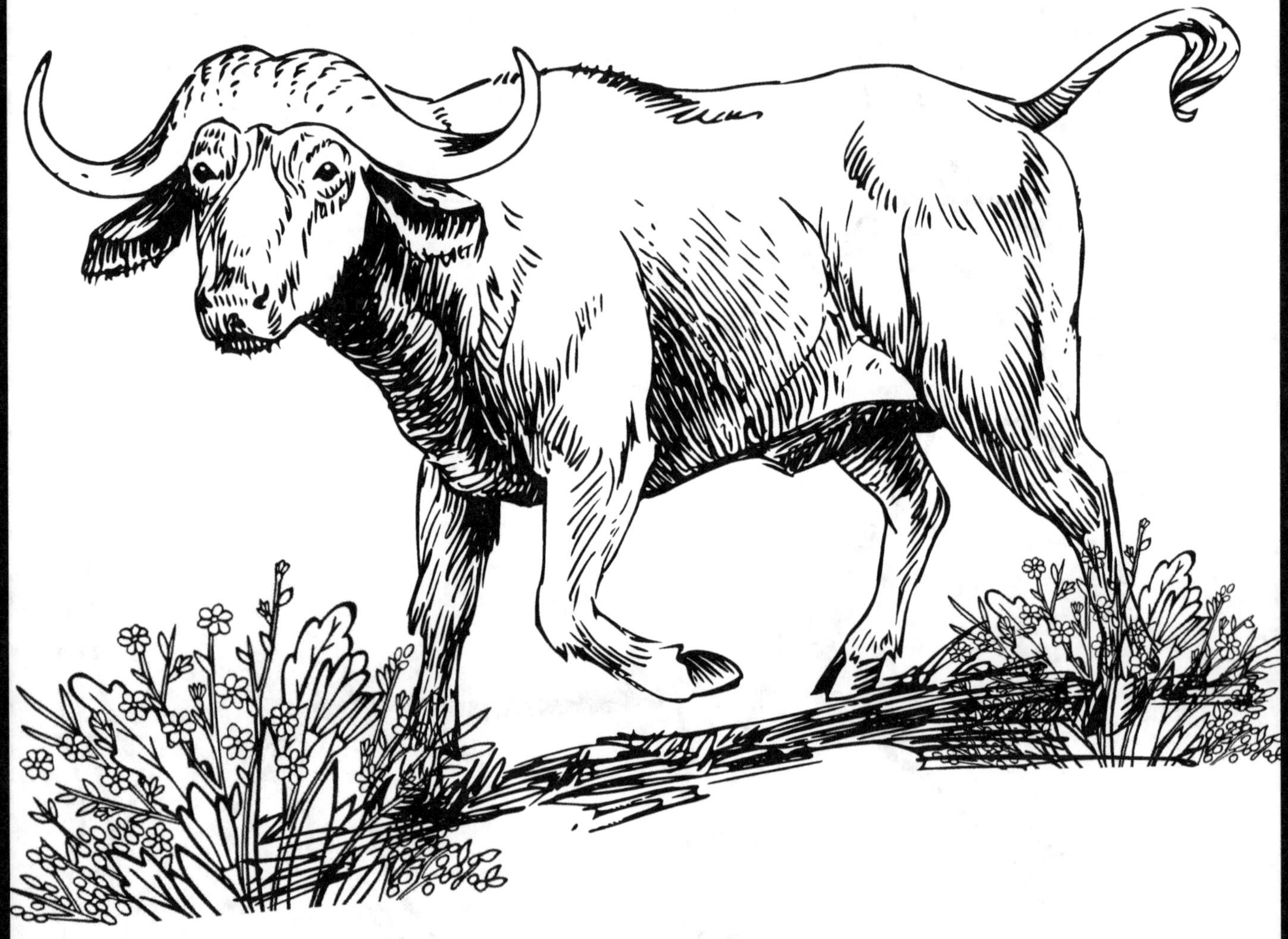

Yak

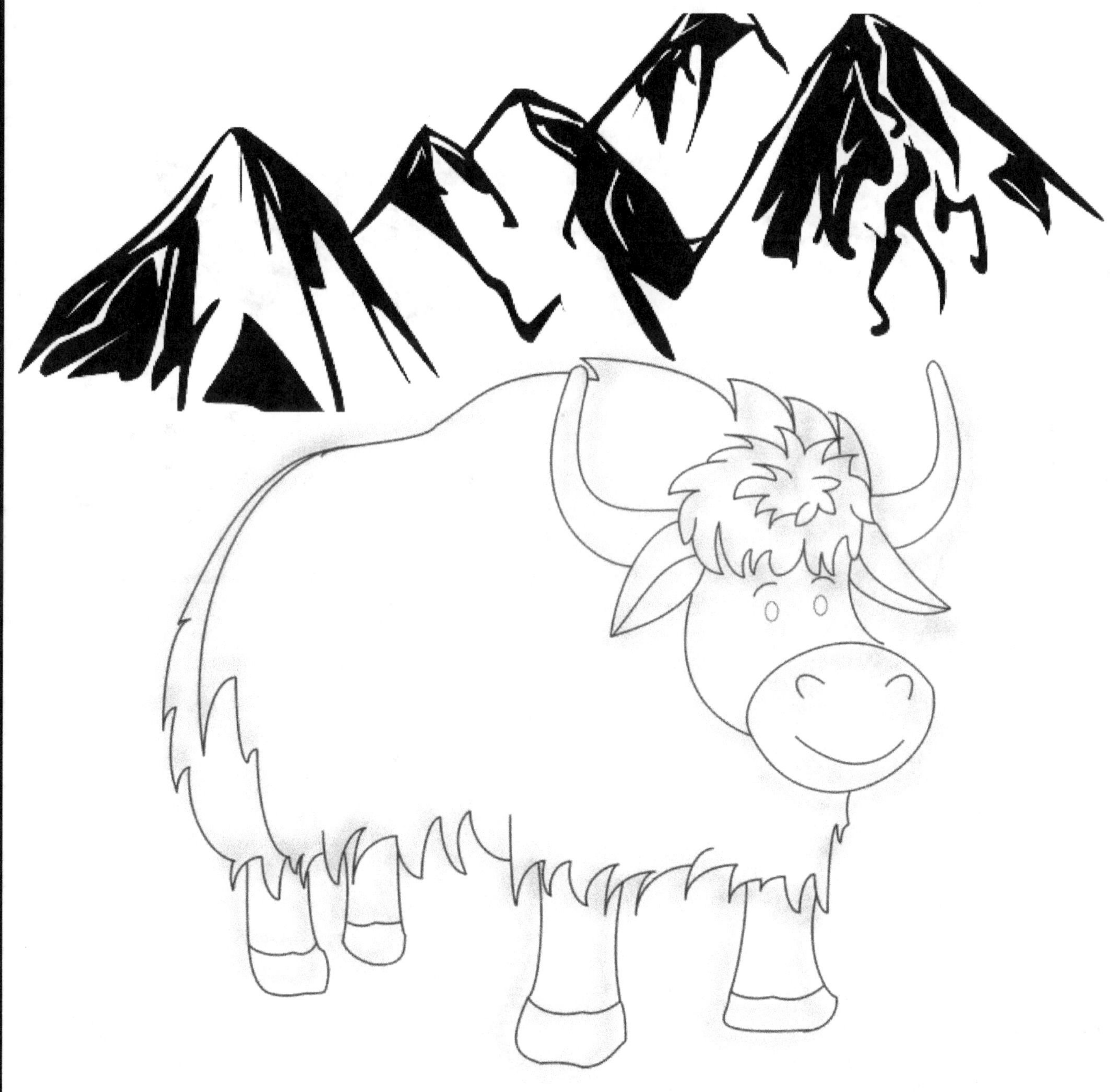

Rhinoceros

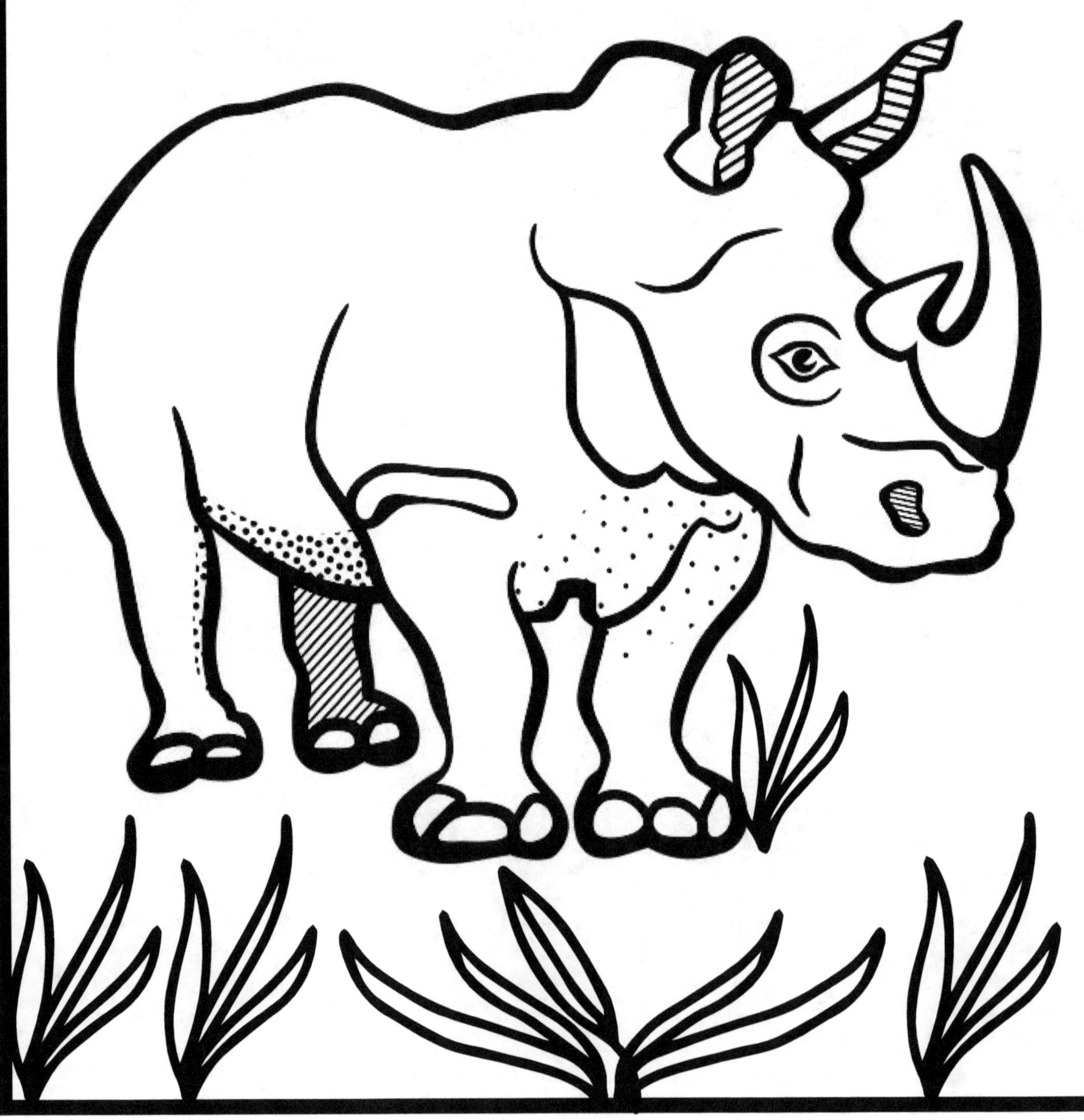

Hippopotamus

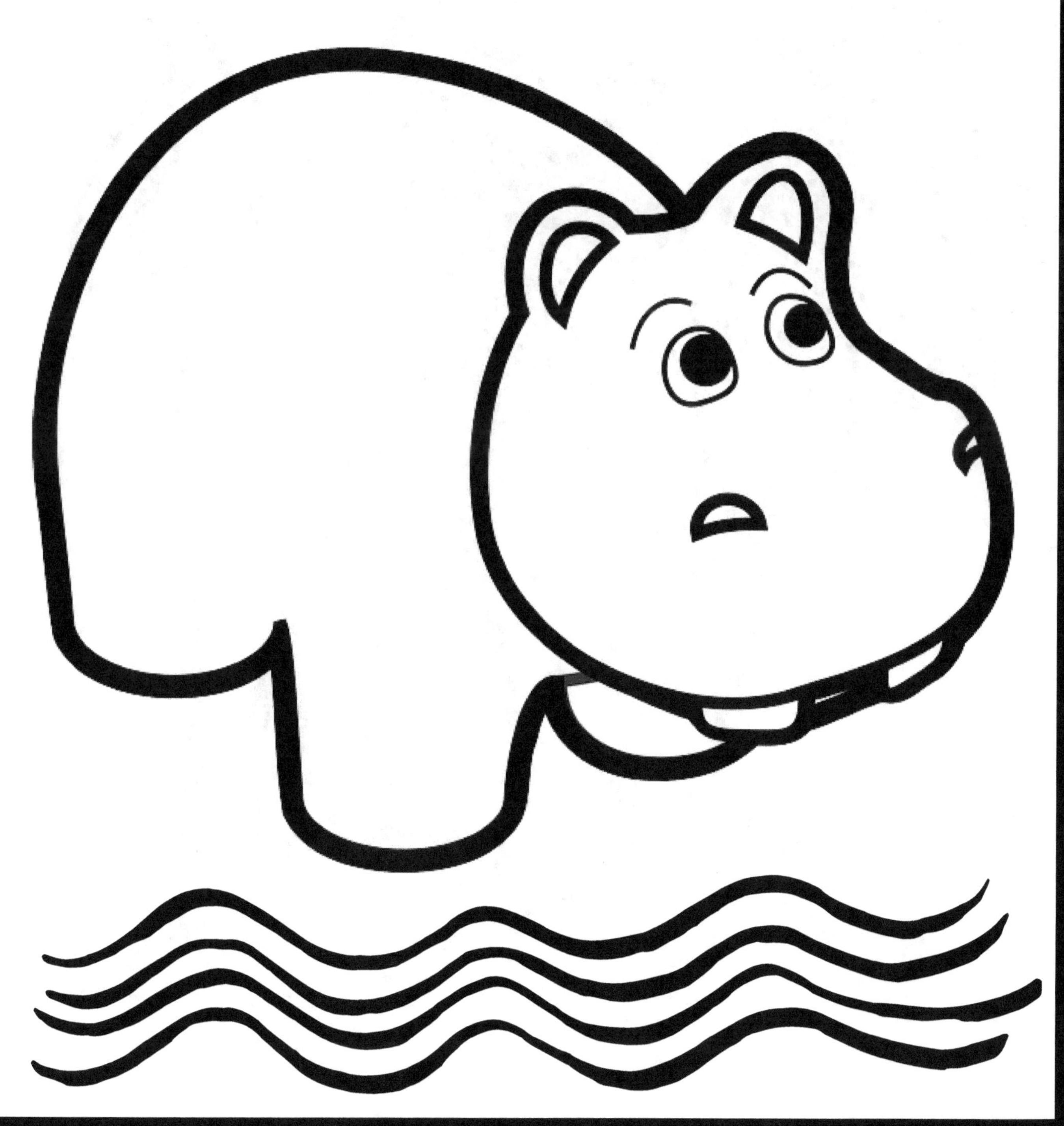

Lion

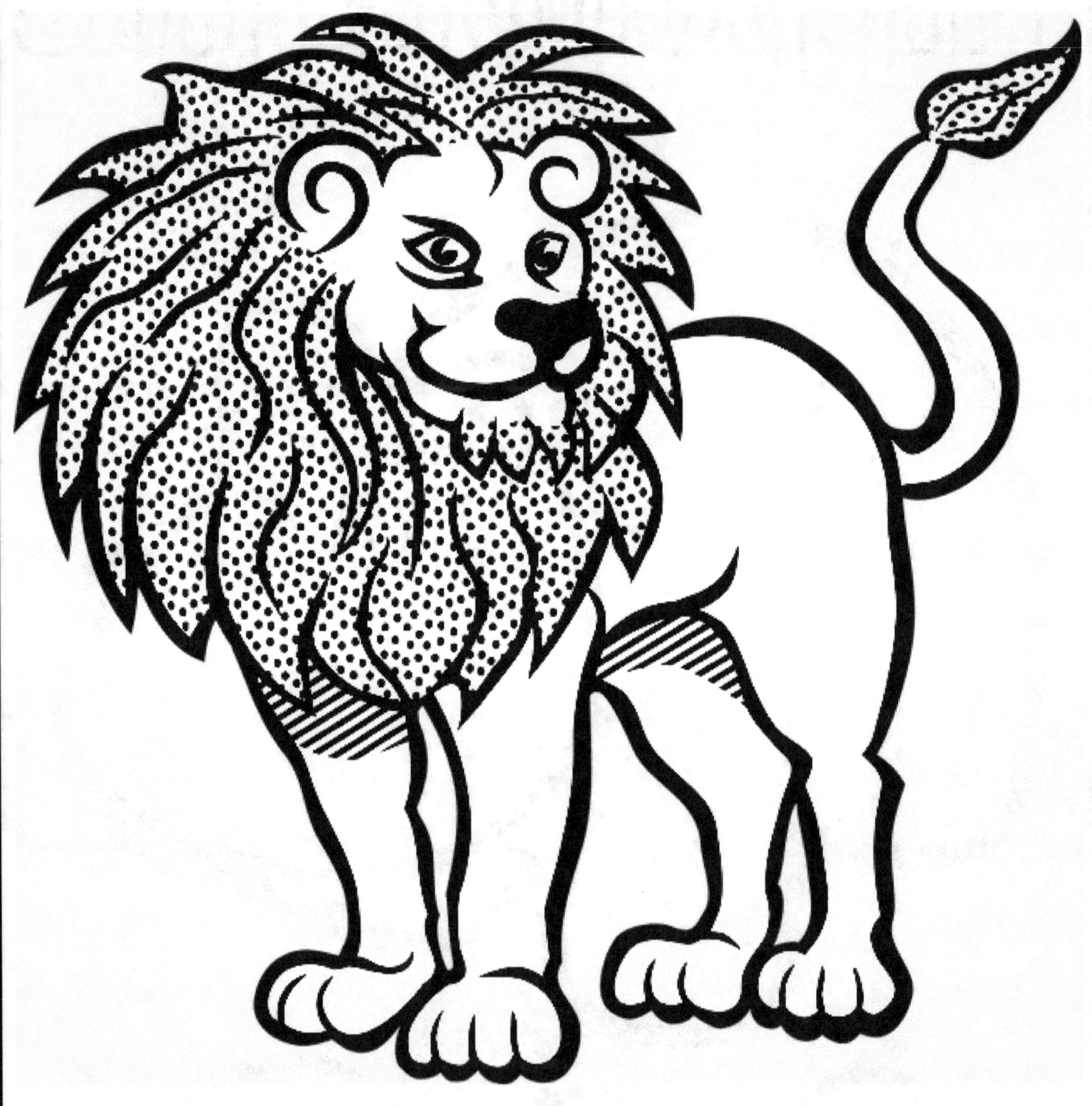

Zebra

Pig

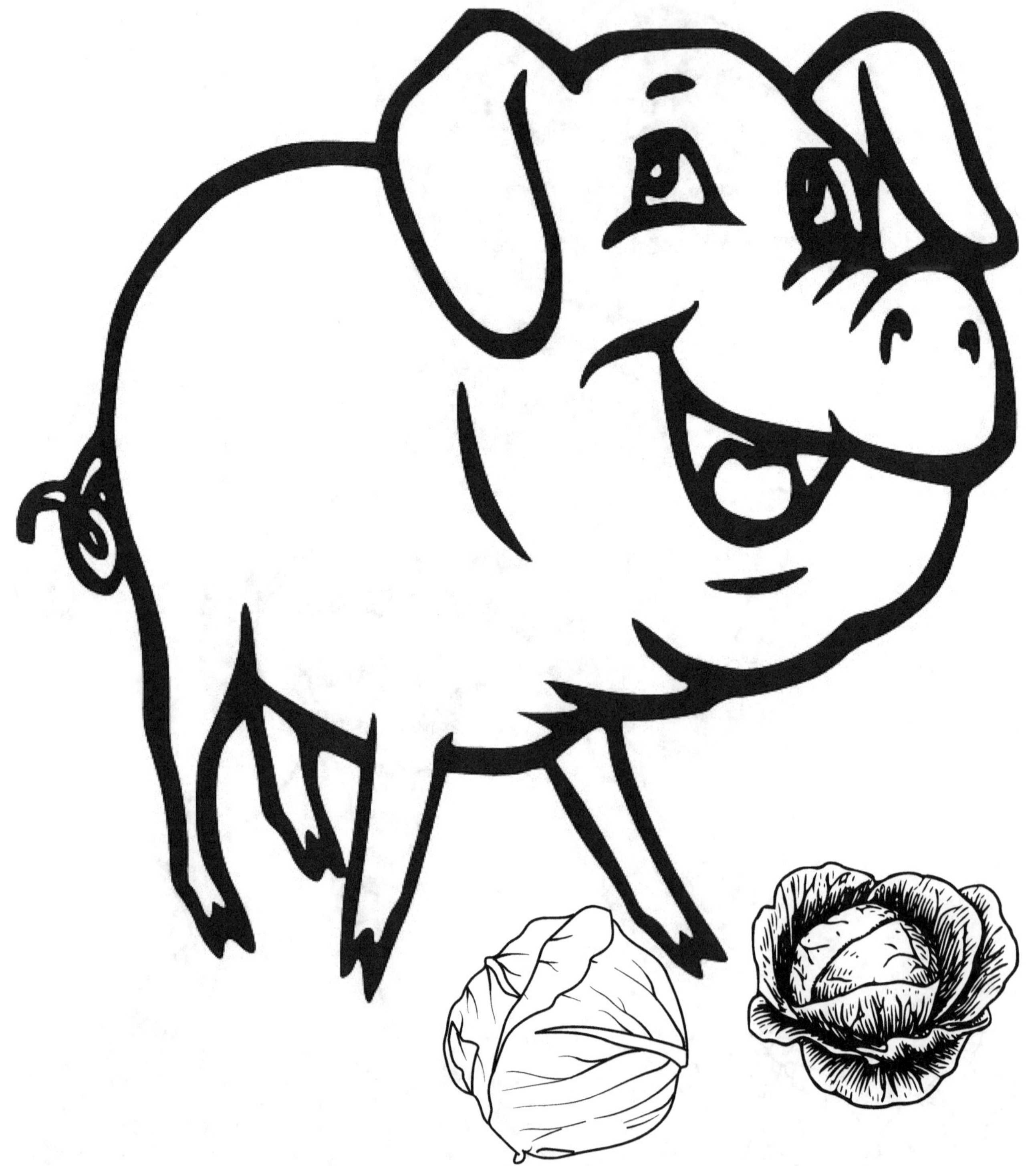

Bear

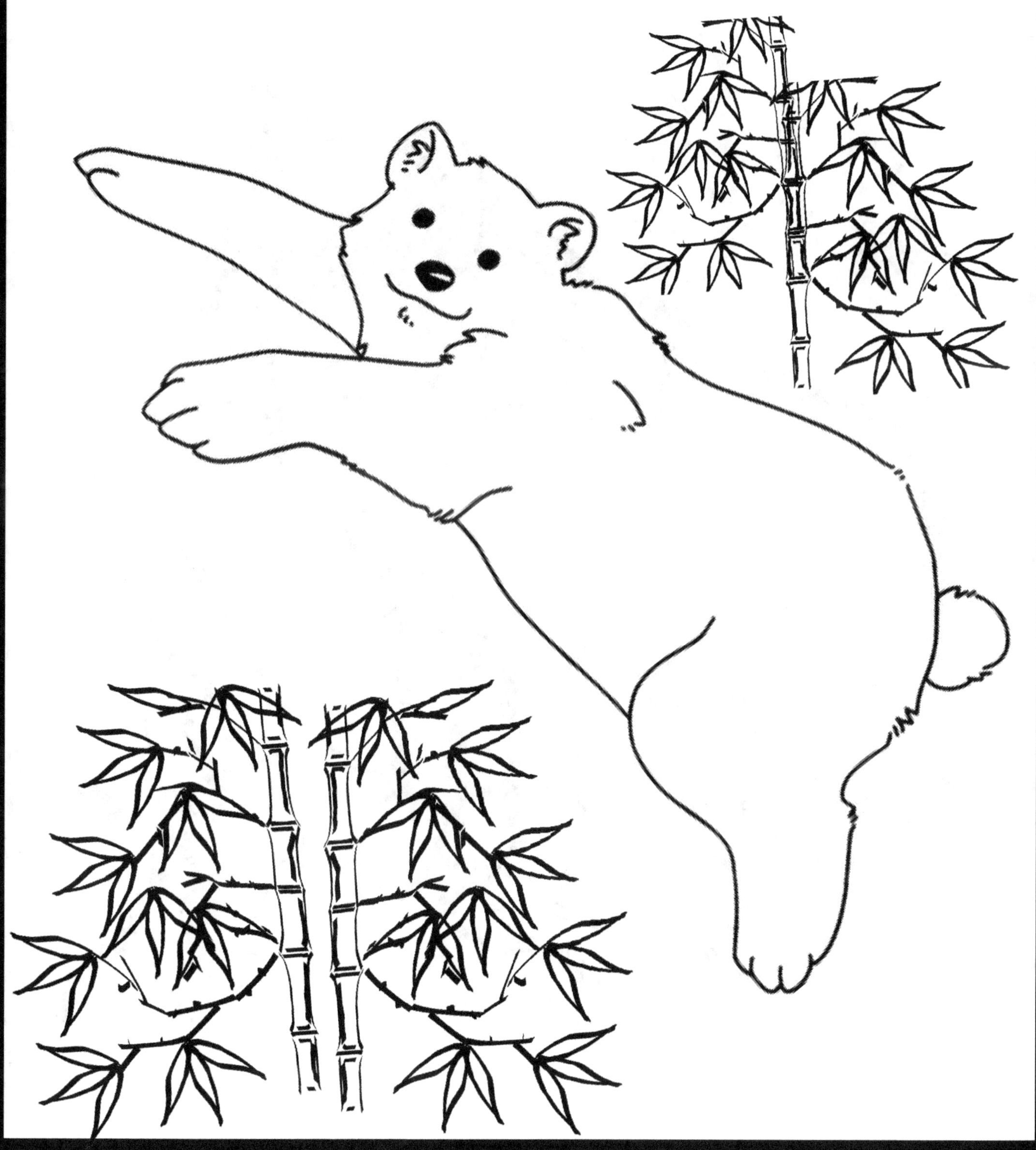

Wolf

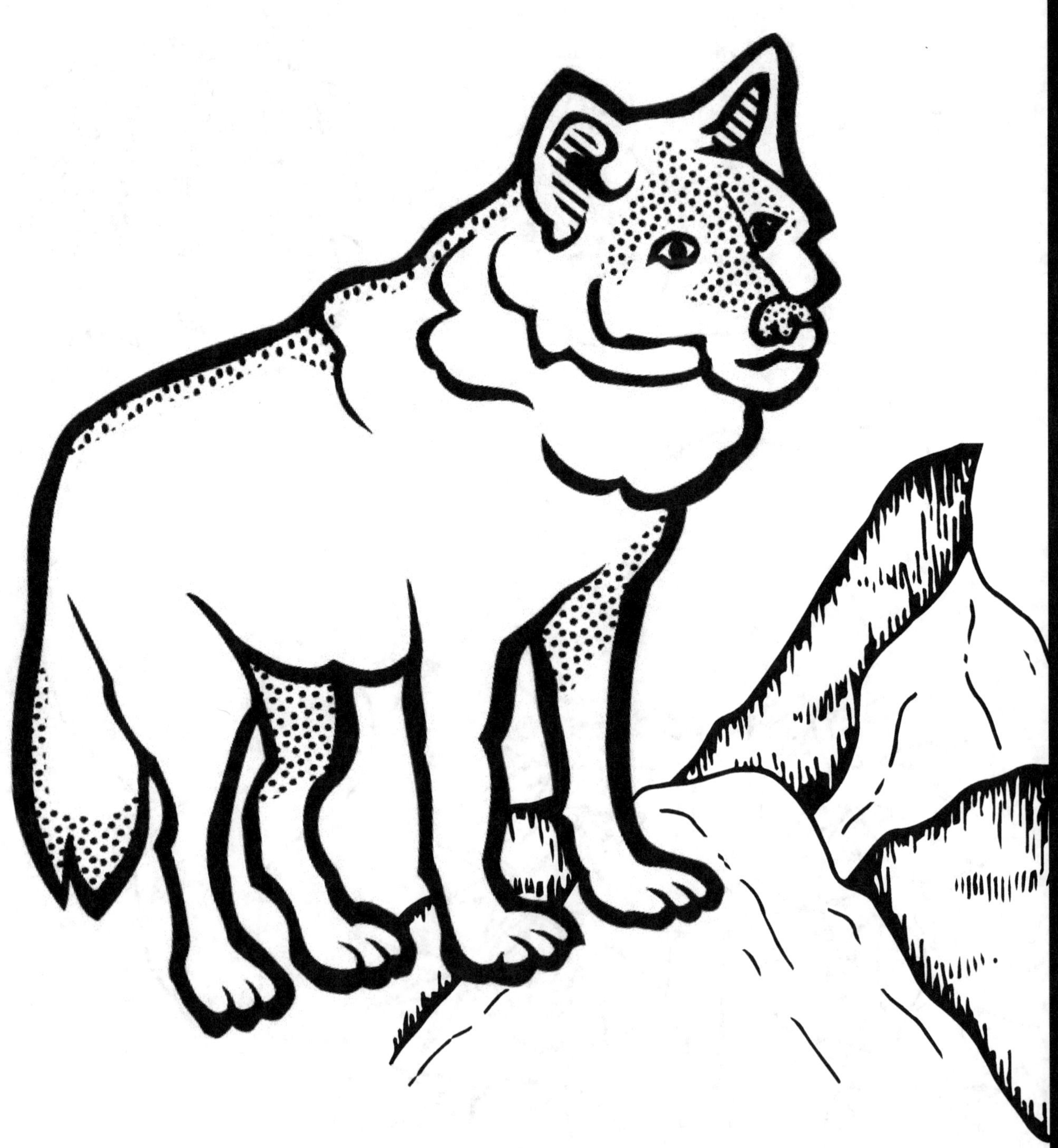

Mouse

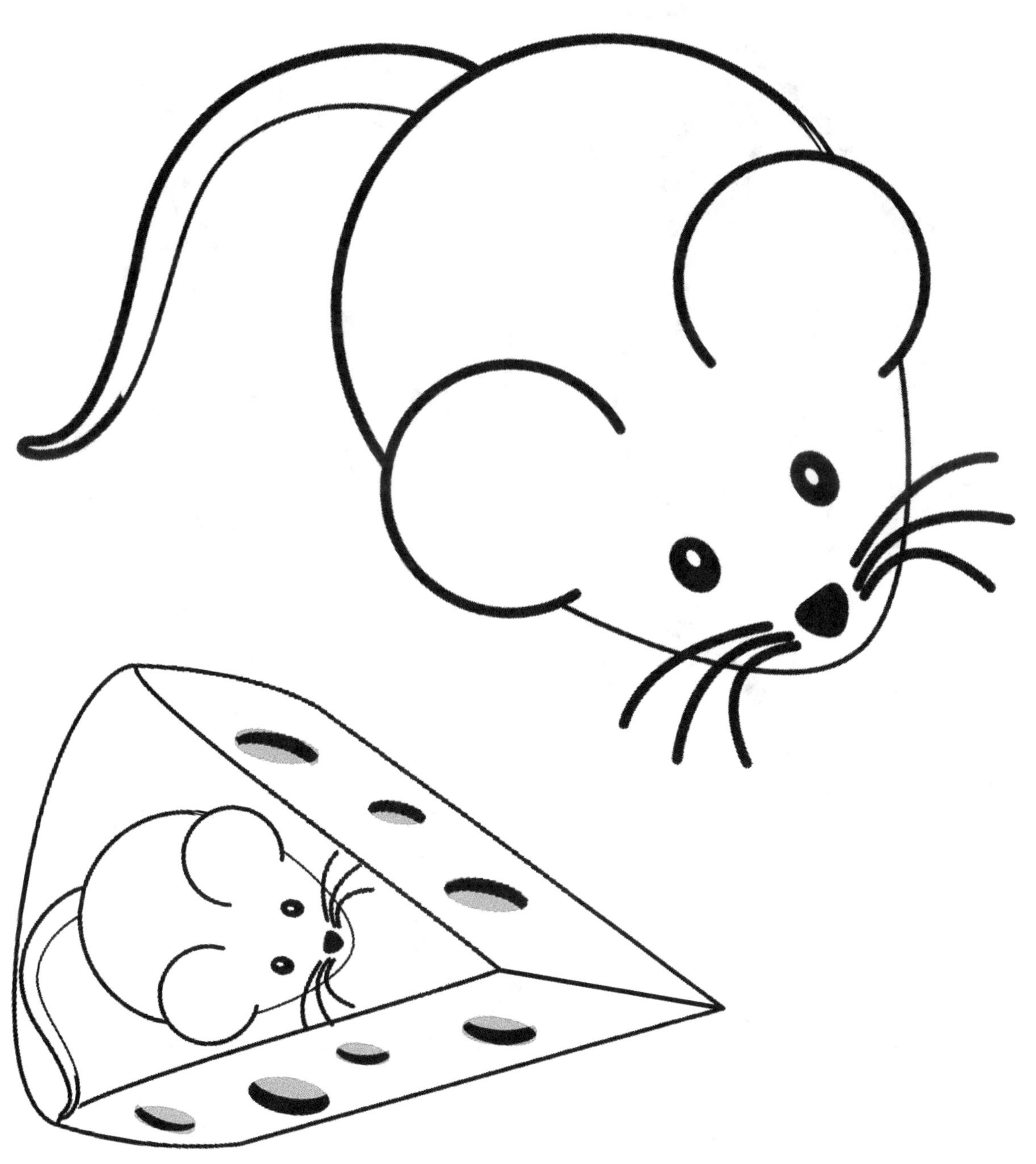

Gorilla

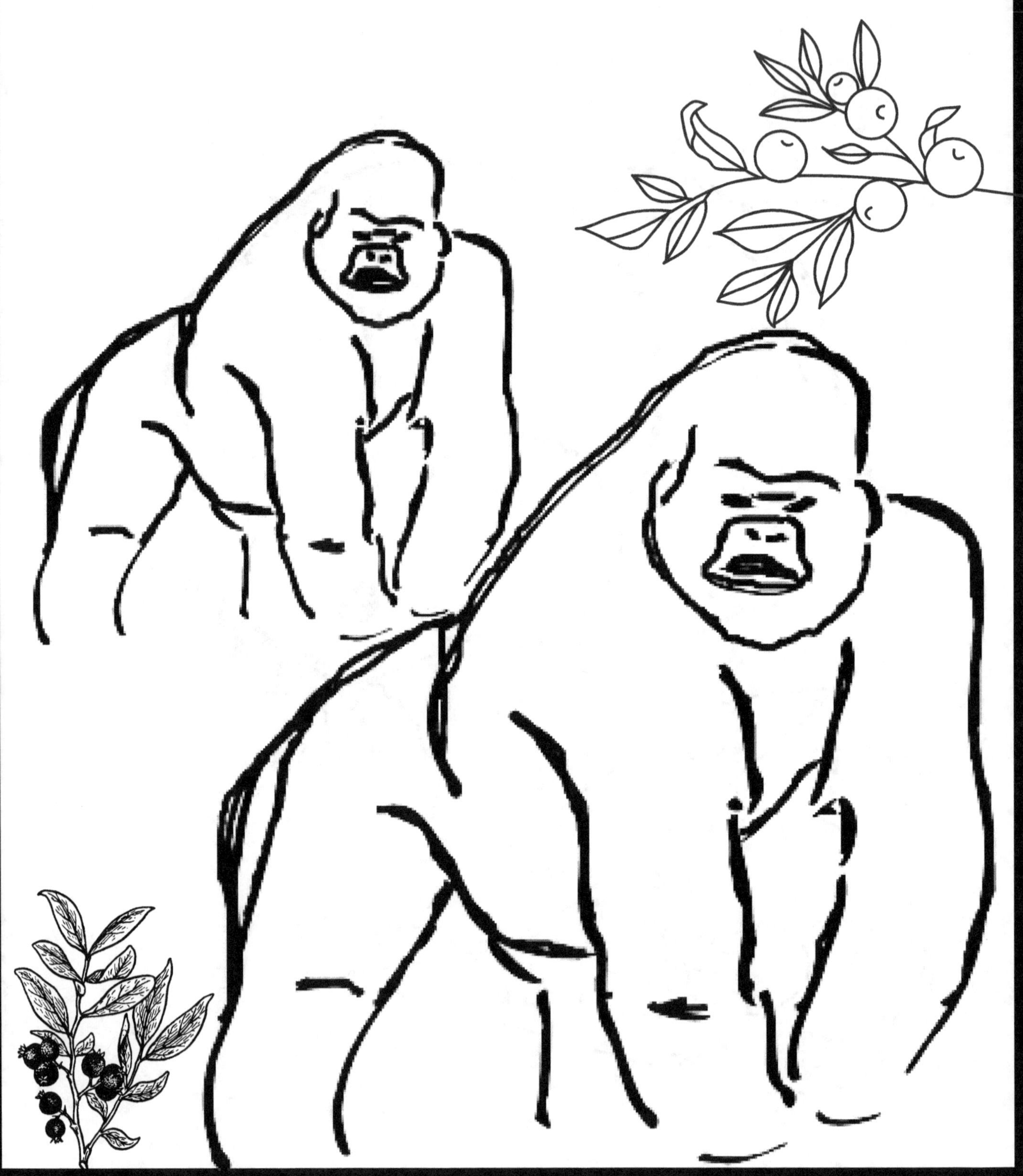

Cow

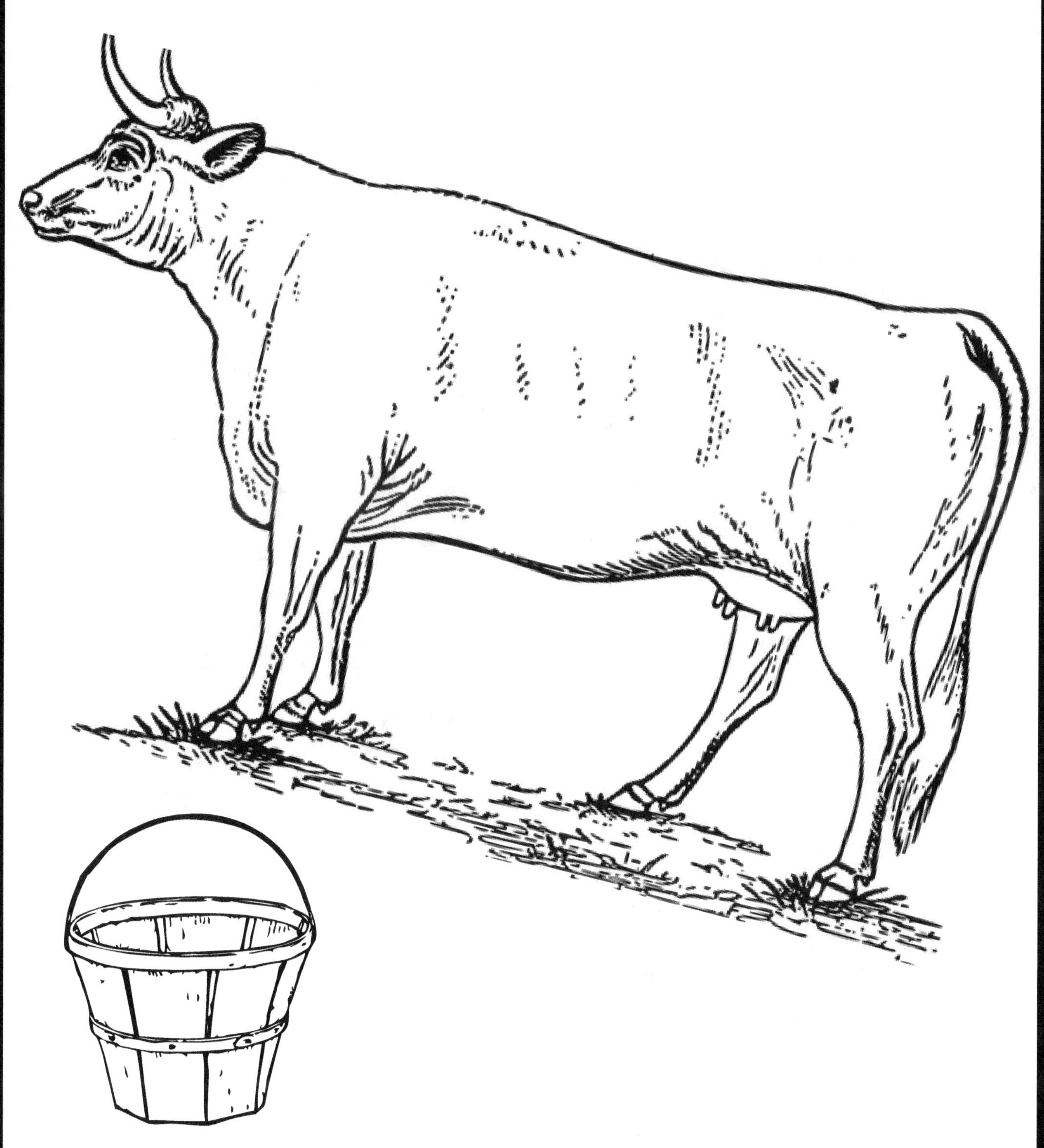

Goat

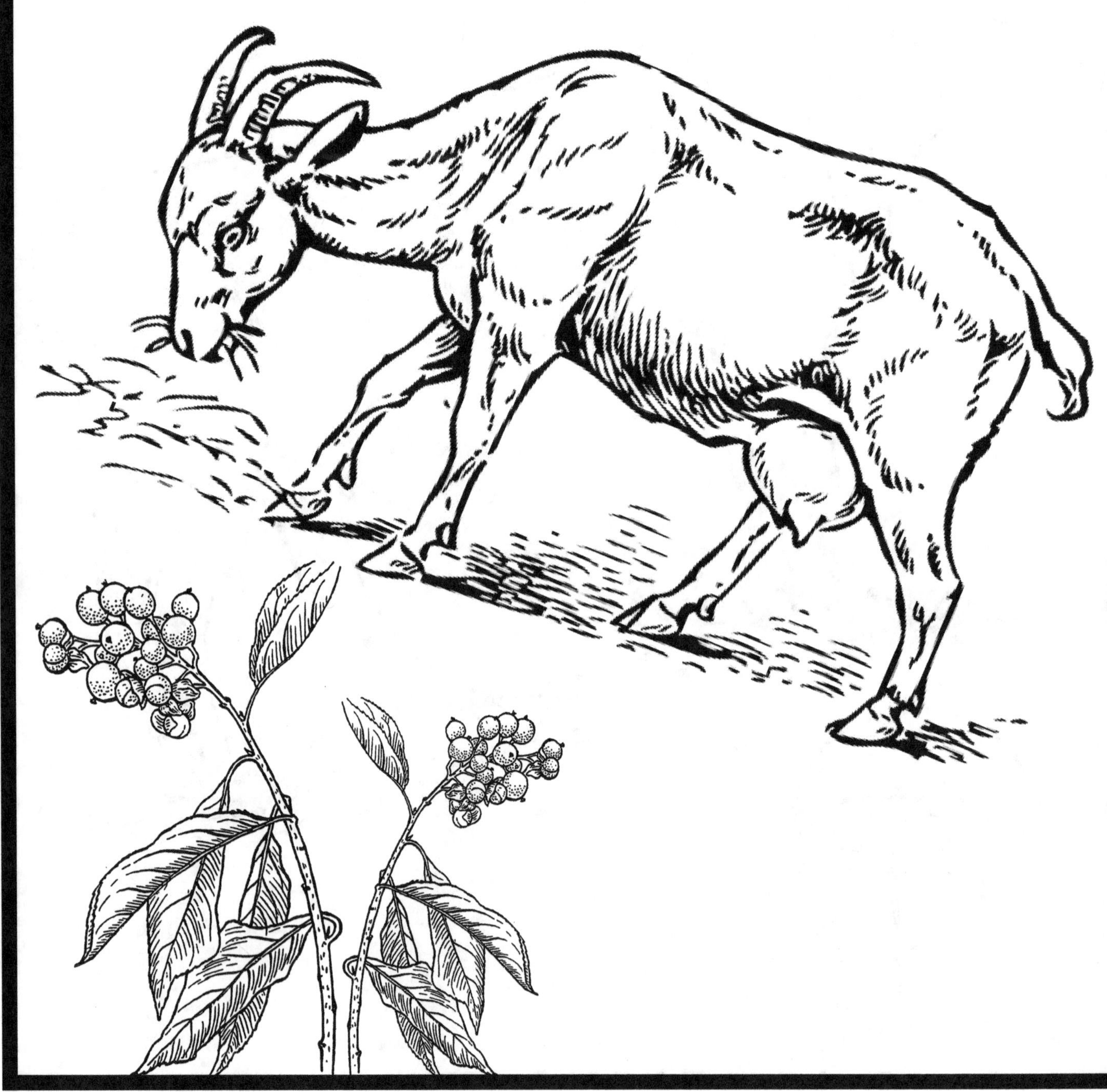

Fox

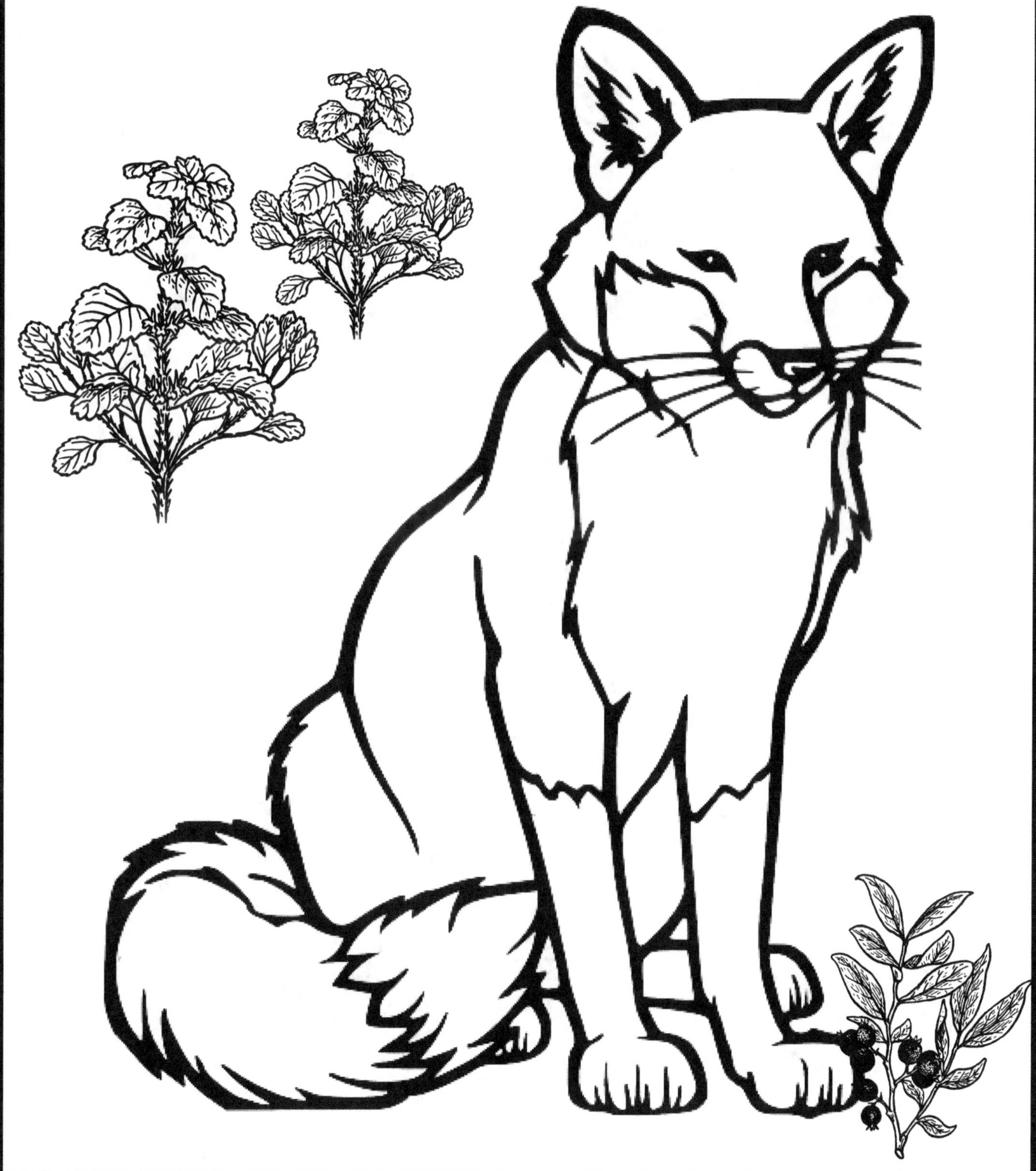

Deer

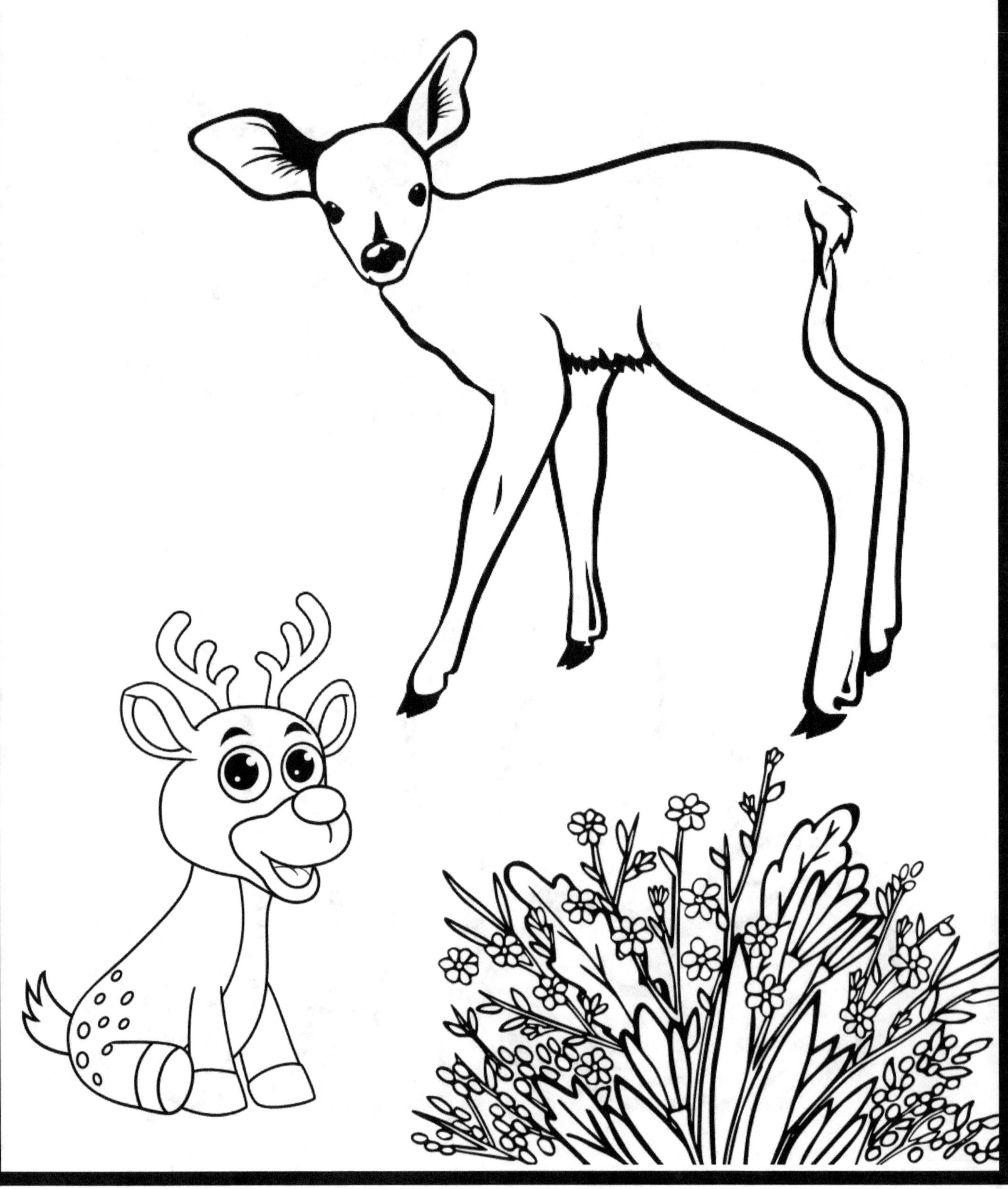

Koala Bear

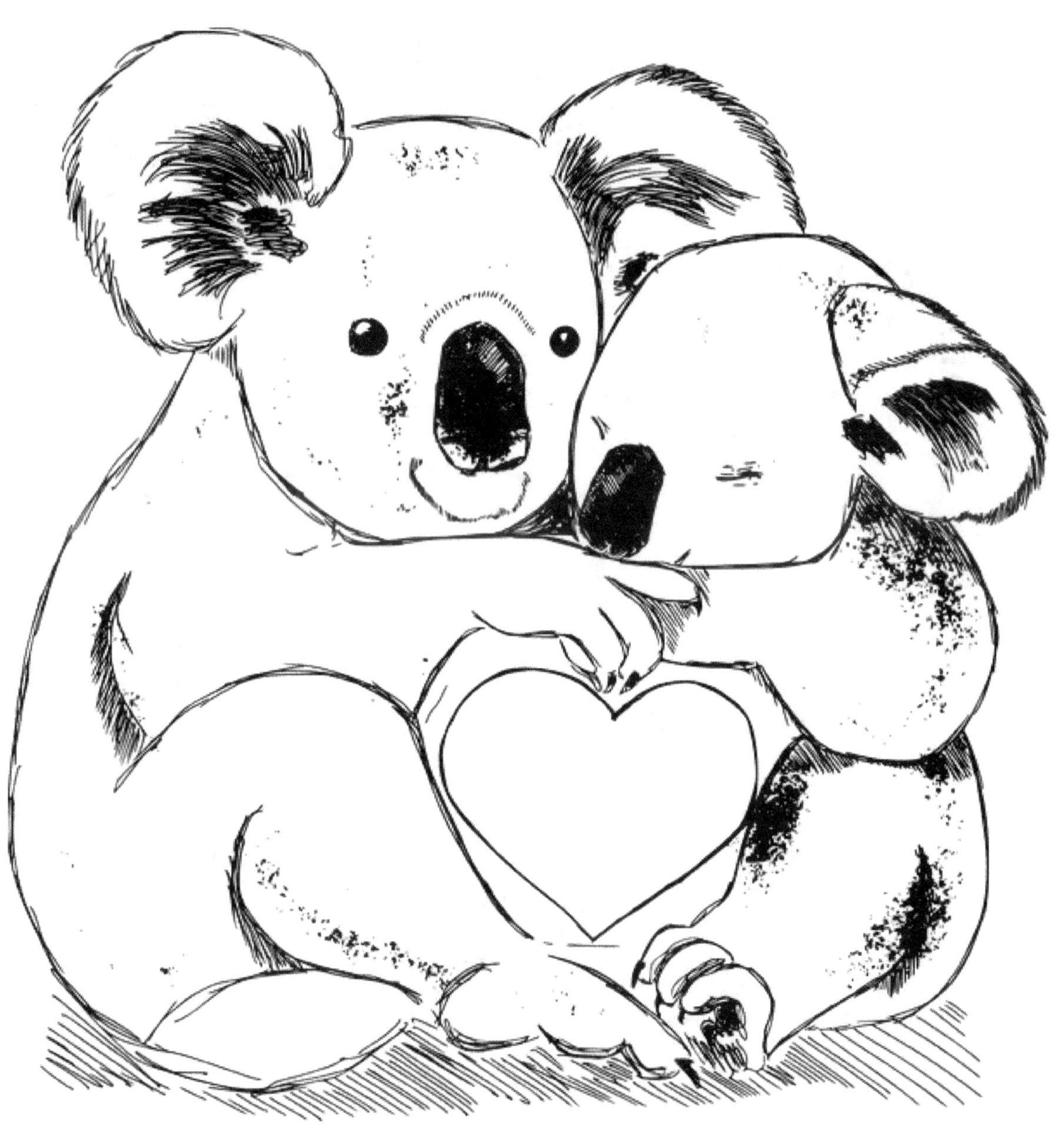

Kangaroo

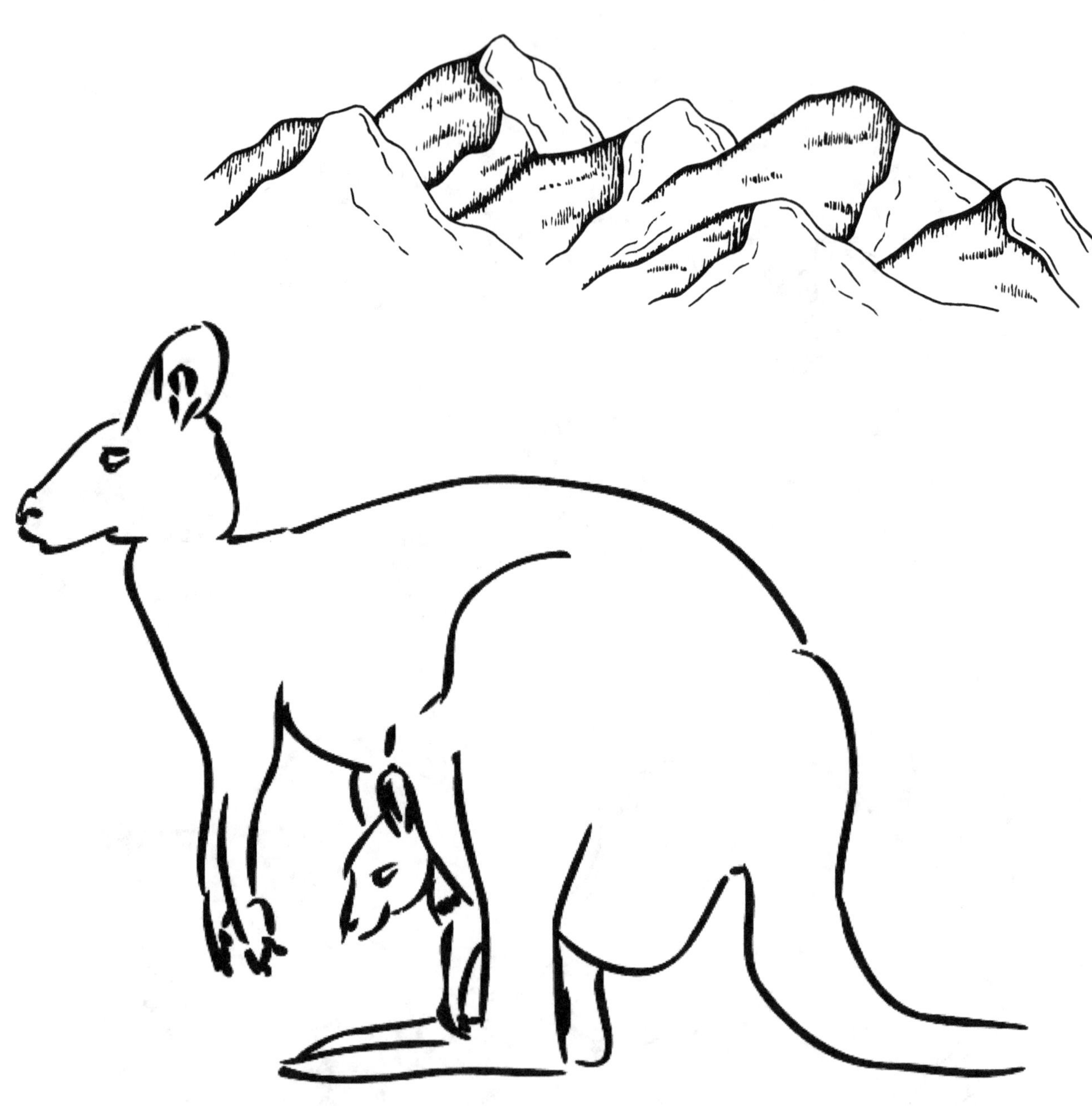

Tiger

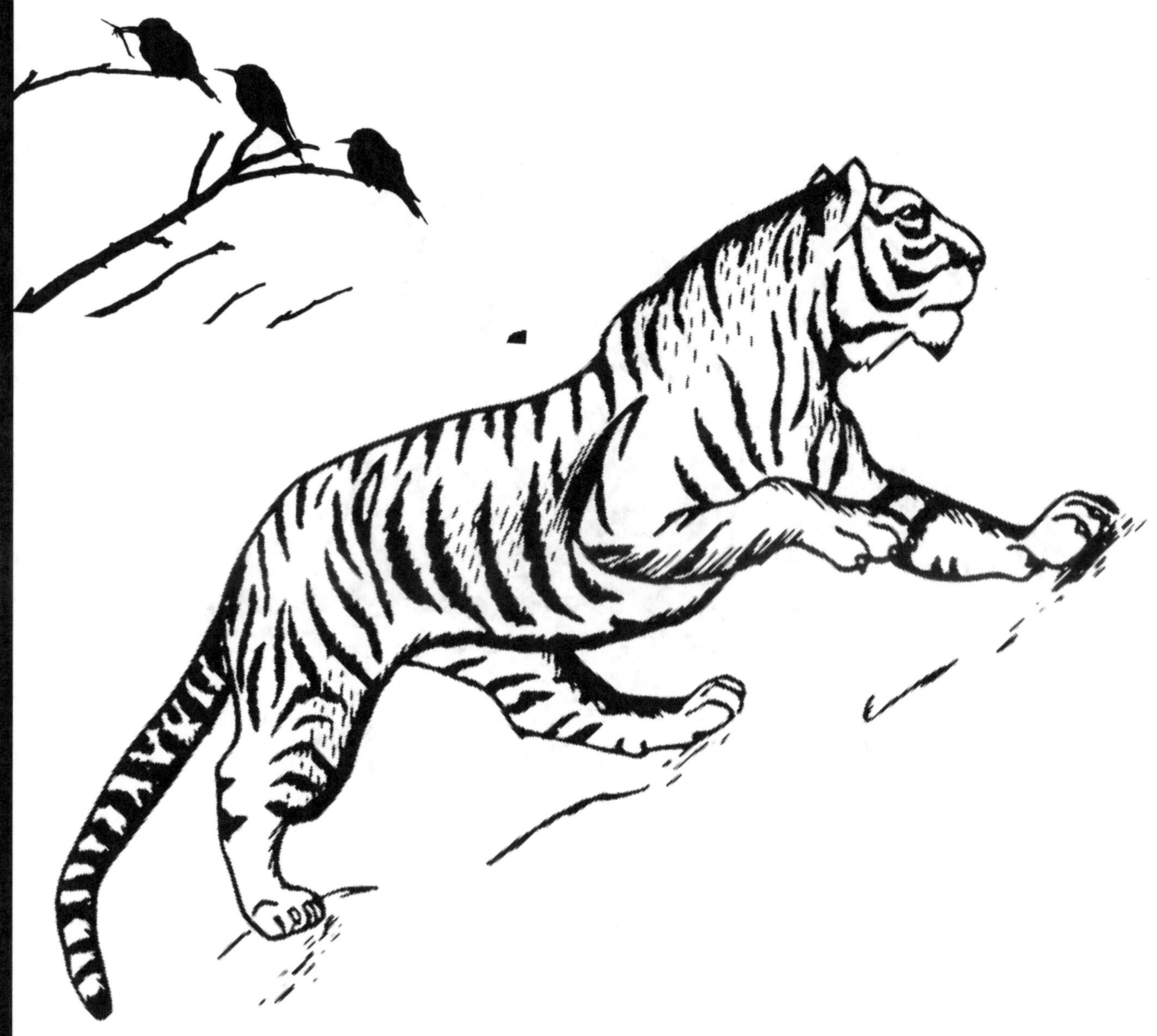

Ant Eater

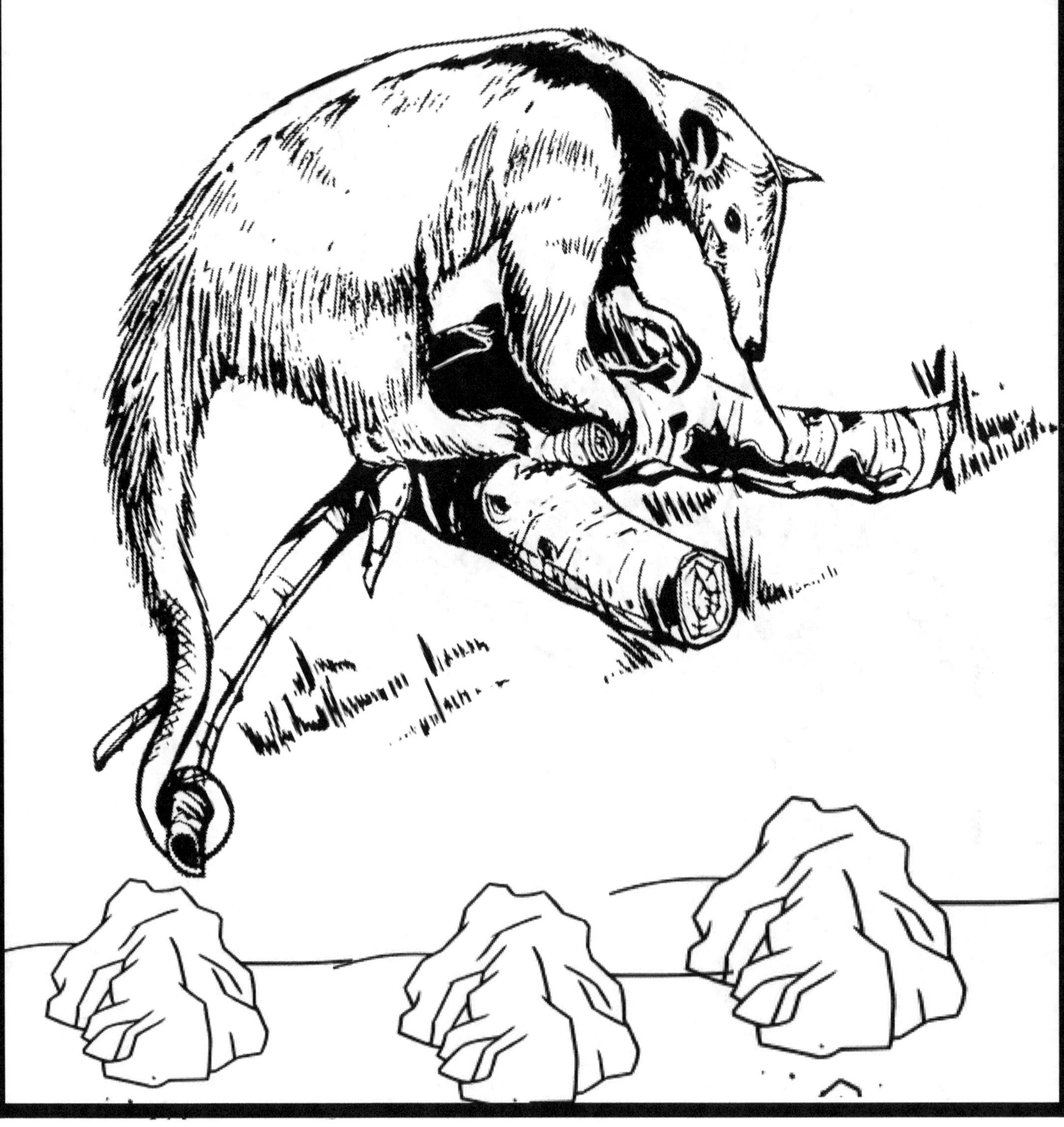

www.ingramcontent.com/pod-product-compliance
Lightning Source LLC
LaVergne TN
LVHW080208180826
845678LV00023BA/1983

* 9 7 8 8 1 9 5 4 8 4 7 3 7 *